PHILIP CAGGIANO was reared in Northport, Long Island, where he began his musical training as a cellist. He began his serious musical study as a voice major at the Juilliard School at the age of sixteen. He is a graduate of New York University. In recent years, Mr. Caggiano has written, directed and designed for opera, theater and film. He lives in New York City. THE RING is his first published theater work.

THE RING
Four Plays for Children

DAS RHEINGOLD
DIE WALKURE
SIEGFRIED
GOTTERDAMMERUNG

Adapted by PHILIP CAGGIANO

*Based on Richard Wagner's music drama,
"Der Ring des Nibelungen"*

A BARD BOOK/PUBLISHED BY AVON BOOKS

AVON BOOKS
A division of
The Hearst Corporation
959 Eighth Avenue
New York, New York 10019

Unpublished manuscript registered for copyright, 1978.
Copyright © 1980 by Philip Caggiano
Published by arrangement with the author
Library of Congress Catalog Card Number: 81-52409
ISBN: 0-380-79434-9

First Bard Printing, March, 1982

BARD TRADEMARK REG. U.S. PAT. OFF. AND IN
OTHER COUNTRIES, MARCA REGISTRADA, HECHO EN
U. S. A.

Printed in the U.S.A.

OP   10   9   8   7   6   5   4   3   2   1

For PHARAOH

CONTENTS

PREFACE

The Ring was first performed by students of the Somers Intermediate School on March 5, 1979, and was subsequently given its New York premiere, with the original Somers children, scenery and costumes, presented by the Wagner Society of New York, at the 92nd Street YM–YWHA Kaufmann Concert Hall, on January 30, 1980. This edition is based on my original direction and production design of *The Ring* in Somers.

When I began to adapt a children's acting version of Richard Wagner's music drama, *Der Ring des Nibelungen*, I had particular ideas in mind: namely, to adapt Wagner's opera cycle into four short children's plays, faithful in narrative fact and placement of musical example, which children could easily perform. In *The Ring*, children are not required to sing. This adaptation is not to be considered an opera, but four related children's plays with musical underscoring using prerecorded orchestral excerpts from Wagner's original operatic score. The only singing, of sorts, is Brunnhilde's *Hojotoho*, where a child playing the part mouths to a recording of a famous interpreter of the Valkyrie heroine. Children play all but three parts: Only the Giants, Fasolt and Fafner, and, in most cases, Wotan should be played by adults.

The production design, as important to me as the adaptation itself, is a children's illustration of what we know to be the current vogue in *Ring* productions. Based on Wieland Wagner's revolutionary Bayreuth staging of 1951,

I stage the action almost entirely on a large disk platform. The disk has two hinged quarters adjusted to various pitches which alter the stage picture. For each of the opera story/ plays, I use one two-dimensional set piece to ornament the appropriate scene or act. So, we see enormous children's booklike cutouts of a castle (modeled after King Ludwig's *Neuschwanstein*) in *Das Rheingold*, an ash tree in *Die Walküre*, Fafner's cave in the second act of *Siegfried*, and a Viking boat for Siegfried and Gunther to sail off in in the first act of *Götterdämmerung*. Only the Rhine River and Nibelheim are played in the orchestra pit, or the area in most school auditoriums between the stage apron and the first row of audience seating. The Rhine is represented by flowing blue fabric, in the style of Chinese theater. In *Das Rheingold*, staging the Rhine and Nibelheim in front of the stage makes it then possible, as Richard Wagner specified, to move from scene to scene in one continuous act without drawing the curtain. The Valhalla scenes fade in and out of view through scrim projections. The Rhine River placement is important in staging *Götterdämmerung*, too, where the Rhine is required in both scenes of Act III. Although I chose to base my physical production after Wieland Wagner's design concept (that his grandfather's stage directions represent "inner visions rather than practical demands," thereby stripping away the use of elaborate sets and staging *The Ring* on a disk abstractly representing the cosmic universe), I have tried to make the stage descriptions here quite general.

The music cues, for the suggested musical excerpts, have been noted within the four plays. The Appendix lists the page and measure numbers coordinated with the G. Schirmer editions of the complete operatic scores, easily available in the United States. There are minute and second timings, as well, useful in timing scene changes. It has been suggested to me, more than once, to use more music. Unfortunately, a soundtrack for these plays must be compiled from commercial recordings or tapes of live broadcast performances. *The Ring*, in its operatic form, is largely sung and wherever you might want to excerpt some additional music—with all due respect to Wagner and Wagnerian singers—it seems to be interrupted by singing. The only way the inclusion of additional underscoring could be possible, short of a recording session with a rather large orchestra, is to play the excerpts on the piano. For what is lost in the orchestral sonorities, I don't recommend it. (It has also been suggested to pull music from other parts of the score and someone once had the deplorable idea of using any music that sounded at all remotely like Wagner.) I gave a great deal of thought to these excerpts and, although I am not about to think that someone may not improve on them, I do believe they are as faithful as this sort of adaptation can be to Wagner's original creation. Out of the ninety minutes it takes to perform *The Ring,* which is performed with one intermission following *Die Walküre,* there are thirty-seven excerpts and nearly forty of the ninety minutes has music playing.

It was my overall intention that *The Ring* would be the *ultimate* children's play. It tells of magic, heroism, legend, good and evil. It is spirited by some of the grandest and most dramatic orchestral music of all time. Children enjoy it, as do their parents, and the rest of us who know and revere Wagner's epic masterpiece have a good time, too.

I would like to express my appreciation to the Somers children, their parents and teachers who gave so enthusiastically toward this project from its onset; to Sarah Hostetter, then Director of Education for the Metropolitan Opera Guild, for having the Guild photograph the Somers children in this first "model" production and later inviting them to perform scenes for the Opera America education workshop in List Hall, at the Metropolitan Opera House, in April 1979; to Stephen Wadsworth, for his flattering article in the November 1979 issue of *Opera News;* to the Wagner Society of New York and Omus Hirshbein, Director of Performing Arts, 92nd Street YM–YWHA Kaufmann Concert Hall, for presenting *The Ring* in its New York premiere; and to Eric Steinman, who taught the plays in all his music classes in Somers and, in the International Year of the Child, produced an uncompromising production of this first children's acting version of Wagner's *Ring*.

—Philip Caggiano

New York City
July 1980

DAS RHEINGOLD

The Rhine Gold

CHARACTERS

THREE RHINEMAIDENS
ALBERICH, *King of the Nibelungs*
WOTAN, *Ruler of the Gods*
FRICKA, *Wife of Wotan, Goddess of Marriage*
FREIA, *Goddess of Youth and Beauty*
FASOLT, *a Giant*
FAFNER, *a Giant*
FROH, *God of Lightning*
DONNER, *God of Thunder*
LOGE, *God of Fire*
MIME, *Brother of Alberich*
ERDA, *The Earth Goddess*
SLAVES

Scene 1: The Depths of the Rhine River

Scene 2: The Mountaintop of the Gods

Scene 3: Nibelheim, Deep in the Earth

Scene 4: The Mountaintop of the Gods

Das Rheingold is performed in one continuous act without drawing the curtain, pause or interruption.

Scene 1: The Depths of the Rhine River

[*Curtain. Music cue 1.*]

Out of the darkness the Rhine River slowly becomes visible, lit in blue-green light. On either side of the river are large craggy rocks. As the river flows, blocks of gold are seen glistening in the center.

[*Enter* RHINEMAIDENS, *one by one, happily swimming around the Gold. Light reveals* ALBERICH *on a rock near the Gold. He watches as the* RHINEMAIDENS *swim.*]

ALBERICH: [*Over music*] What are you pretty ladies doing?

RHINEMAIDEN I: What's it to you?

RHINEMAIDEN II: Why would someone ugly like you want to know?
[*The* RHINEMAIDENS *continue to swim around the Rhine Gold.*]

ALBERICH: Come closer, it's hard for me to talk to you when you're swimming around.

RHINEMAIDEN III: No! Stay away you ugly hairy thing!

ALBERICH: [*More insistently*] Tell me what you are doing, swimming around all day?

RHINEMAIDEN I: We're the Rhinemaidens. Our father says we must protect the Rhine Gold.

ALBERICH: [*With growing curiosity*] What's so important about the Rhine Gold?

RHINEMAIDEN II: One day a ring will be made from the Gold.

RHINEMAIDEN III: Its owner will then be able to rule the world.

17

RHINEMAIDEN I: But *only* someone willing to give up love forever.

[ALBERICH *climbs to where the Rhine Gold rests.*]

ALBERICH: [*Holding the Gold above him*] I will give up love forever! *I* will become master of the world!

[ALBERICH *snatches the Gold and escapes from the reach of the* RHINEMAIDENS. *Exit* ALBERICH, *into the depths, where he quickly disappears.*]

RHINEMAIDENS: [*Hollering after him*] Come back here with our Gold! You ugly little monster! You've stolen our Gold! *(etc.)*

[ALBERICH's *mocking laughter is heard from off stage. Lights fade as the* RHINEMAIDENS *continue to holler after* ALBERICH. *Music fades.*]

END OF SCENE 1

Scene 2: The Mountaintop of the Gods

[*Music cue 2.*]

Through the mist, light reveals the glimmering new castle, Valhalla. To the other side of the stage are WOTAN *and* FRICKA, *standing on the mountaintop admiring their new home. Music fades.*

WOTAN: Well Fricka, are you happy with your new home? Those two Giants, Fasolt and Fafner, certainly have built a castle worthy of the Gods.

FRICKA: Well, I suppose I'm happy that it's finally done. But, I haven't forgotten that you promised my dear sister Freia as payment.

WOTAN: That is the price we agreed on.

FRICKA: The price is too high! My poor sister, the Goddess

of Youth and Beauty, having to spend the rest of her days with those two. For vain power you have let this happen.

WOTAN: To win you, Fricka, I gladly gave up one of my eyes. [*Gesturing to the patch he wears over one eye*] I will not abandon Freia.

[*Enter* FREIA, *running to the protection of* WOTAN.]

FREIA: [*Very frightened*] Wotan... Fricka... please help me. The Giants are on their way to take me as payment for your castle.

WOTAN: Wait Freia, Loge will be here any moment. He tells me that he might have a plan to offer them something else.

[*Music cue* 3. *Enter the Giants,* FASOLT *and* FAFNER.]

FASOLT: Wotan, we are here to collect our payment for the construction of your castle.

WOTAN: One moment, gentlemen, I'll be right with you. Loge will be here any moment. He always advises me on affairs of state. Perhaps while you are waiting you might think of a payment you would rather have than my sister-in-law.

FASOLT: No other! Freia alone!

FAFNER: [*Showing* WOTAN *the contract*] We have the contract right here, Wotan.

FASOLT: You are the chief God. You have sworn on your spear. You have to keep your word. So, we'll just take the little lady with us right now.

FREIA: [*Pleading*] Please, Wotan, please...

[*Enter* FROH *and* DONNER.]

FROH: I will shield you, sister!

DONNER: Fasolt, Fafner, you do not know the weight of my hammer!

[*Enter* LOGE.]

WOTAN: [*Aside to* LOGE] Loge, you told me you would find a way to get me out of this building contract. My wife is furious that I'm selling her sister off to these house builders.

LOGE: Well, they have finished their job and really are entitled to collect their fee. I've been traveling around and I can't find anything that would be a good substitute. There is, of course, the Rhine Gold.

GIANTS: [*Having overheard them*] The Rhine Gold?

FREIA: The Rhine Gold?

FRICKA: The Rhine Gold?

LOGE: Yes, the Rhine Gold. But, wouldn't you know, Alberich stole it, renounced love, forged a ring from the Gold, and now plans to rule the world.

WOTAN: Didn't I assign the Rhinemaidens to look after it?

LOGE: Yes, but that awful dwarf stole it.

FRICKA: [*Caressingly to* WOTAN] Oh, might my *husband* win back the Gold?

DONNER: [*To the other* GODS] We would all be slaves to Alberich if the Ring is not returned.

FAFNER: I'll tell you what, Wotan. Fasolt and I would settle for the Rhine Gold in place of Freia.

WOTAN: The Rhine Gold? *Never!*

[*Exit* FASOLT *and* FAFNER, *dragging* FREIA *off. As* FREIA's *plea for help is heard in the distance, a pale mist fills the stage. The* GODS *look at one another and see that they are all growing old. Horrified that they, as Gods, will age without the presence of the Goddess of Youth and Beauty, implore* WOTAN *to help.*]

LOGE: [*Touching his face*] Wotan, look at us! We are all growing old. Without Freia, the Goddess of Youth and Beauty, we Gods are all doomed to mortal old age.

EVERYONE: [*All touching their faces*] Please Wotan...We can't face old age...Do something...I can feel the wrinkles happening...Please...(*etc.*)

WOTAN: Very well. I will go to Nibelheim, down deep in the earth. I will find that dreadful Alberich, recover the Rhine Gold and return to ransom Freia!

[*Blackout. Music cue 4.*]

END OF SCENE 2

Scene 3: Nibelheim, Deep in the Earth

[*Lights up.*]

In the gloomy cavern inhabited by the Nibelungs, MIME *is at work forging a helmet of Gold. He works at a crude rock at center, hammering in time to the music. Music fades.*

[*Enter* ALBERICH.]

ALBERICH: Why haven't you finished forging the invisible helmet? I'll have to beat you again if your work doesn't improve.

MIME: [*Exhausted*] Alberich, I'm almost finished.

ALBERICH: [*Examining* MIME'*s work*] It's already finished! I see, you wanted to keep it for yourself. Selfish monster! I'll teach you to try and fool me. [*Whips him*]
[*Exit* ALBERICH. *Enter* WOTAN *and* LOGE. *They come upon* MIME, *he is crying.*]

WOTAN: Poor fellow, what's wrong?

MIME: Alberich beat me. He said I tried to deceive him with the Tarnhelm. Ever since he forged the magic Ring he has made all our lives miserable. This used to be a jolly place. Now it is like a sweatshop. We have to rest . . . night or day.
[*Enter* ALBERICH, *leading a horde of* SLAVES. *The* SLAVES *carry blocks of the Gold. As they go,* ALBERICH *whips them.* ALBERICH *pauses and sees* WOTAN *and* LOGE, *then hurries the* SLAVES *away. Exit* MIME *with* SLAVES.]

ALBERICH: [*To* WOTAN *and* LOGE] What are you doing here?

WOTAN: We heard about all your newfound treasures.

LOGE: We wanted to see the treasures for ourselves. What is your secret?

ALBERICH: My *Gold!*

LOGE: What would happen if someone were to steal the Gold and the Ring?

ALBERICH: I have the Tarnhelm. When I wear it I can disappear or take any shape I desire.

LOGE: I don't believe it. Show us.

[ALBERICH *puts on the Tarnhelm and vanishes. A large serpent appears.* WOTAN *and* LOGE *pretend to be terrified.* ALBERICH *regains his human form.*]

ALBERICH: What do you think of that?

WOTAN: A serpent is easy. Any magician can do that.

LOGE: Can you change yourself into something small? Perhaps . . . a toad?

[ALBERICH *vanishes and a toad is seen on the nearby rock.* WOTAN *spots the toad, crosses and carefully steps on it.* LOGE *seizes the toad and ties it up.* ALBERICH, *tied up, regains his human form.* WOTAN *and* LOGE *take* ALBERICH *as their prisoner.*]

ALBERICH: [*As he is taken off*] Curse you . . . Curse you both . . . Curse you . . . (*etc.*)

[*Exit* WOTAN, LOGE *and* ALBERICH. *Music cue 5. Lights fade.*]

END OF SCENE 3

Scene 4: The Mountaintop of the Gods

Clouds and mist all but obscure the castle.

[*Lights up as Music fades. Enter* WOTAN, LOGE *and* ALBERICH.]

ALBERICH: [*As he is led on*] Curse you . . . Let me go . . . Curse you . . . (*etc.*)

WOTAN: Alberich, you may buy your freedom . . . with the *Gold*.

ALBERICH: [*Aside*] As long as I have the Ring I can replenish the Gold. [*To* LOGE] Loosen my hand.

[LOGE *unties* ALBERICH'*s hand who then raises the Ring to his lips, summoning his* SLAVES *to deliver the Gold.*] Slaves! Slaves! Bring me my Gold!

[*Enter* SLAVES, *they carry in blocks of the Gold, set them down upstage and exit.* LOGE *takes the Tarnhelm from* ALBERICH.] You greedy scoundrels! Don't think you have tricked me. I can have Mime make me another.

LOGE: [*To* WOTAN] Can we release the prisoner now?

WOTAN: First I must have the Ring.

ALBERICH: [*Trembling*] The Ring! My life, but not the Ring!

WOTAN: Give me the Ring! With your life . . . do what you will.

ALBERICH: Who ever takes this Ring is doomed forever.

[WOTAN, *ignoring him, violently tears the Ring from* AL-BERICH'*s hand.*]

ALBERICH: [*Falling to his knees with a horrible cry*] Ah . . . I am defeated!

WOTAN: [*Contemplating the Ring*] This Ring now lifts me on high. The mightiest Lord of all might. [*He puts on the Ring.*]

[LOGE *sets* ALBERICH *free.*]

ALBERICH: [*As he exits*] The Ring will bring death to all who own it. You can never escape the Ring's curse!

[*Exit* ALBERICH. *Enter* FRICKA, DONNER *and* FROH.]

FRICKA: Wotan, you have brought us good news?

LOGE: By cunning and force the task is done. [*Gesturing to the Gold*] Here is Freia's ransom.

[*Enter* FREIA, *to the arms of* FRICKA.]

FRICKA: Lovely sister, given to us again.

[*Enter* FASOLT *and* FAFNER.]

FASOLT: *Not yet!* She is still ours!

WOTAN: Gentlemen. . . . Your ransom is here. I have the Rhine Gold for you.

FAFNER: This must be an even trade, Wotan. The Gold must be equal in size to Freia. Pile up the Gold so there is enough to hide her completely.

LOGE: Help me Froh.

[LOGE *and* FROH *pile up the blocks of Gold to hide* FREIA.]

FAFNER: [*Instructing* LOGE *and* FROH] Don't pile the Gold loosely. Fill up those crannies. Still more.... Pile on still more.

DONNER: I can't stand it!

FAFNER: Patience Donner. Your thunder does not help you here.

DONNER: [*Raising his mighty hammer*] It will... to crush you!

WOTAN: [*Raising his spear*] Peace! Freia is hidden.

FAFNER: I can still see Freia's hair. [*Pointing to the Tarnhelm*] Throw on that, too.

[LOGE *holds the Tarnhelm up to* WOTAN.]

WOTAN: [*Sadly*] Let it go, too.

[LOGE *places the Tarnhelm on top of the pile*.]

FASOLT: I can see Freia's eyes.

FAFNER: You must add the *Ring!*

WOTAN: No! No! Not the Ring!

FREIA: Help me, help me!

FRICKA: Cruel God, give up the Ring!

DONNER: Give them the Ring!

FROH: Don't hold back the Gold!

[*Music cue* 6. *Enter* ERDA, *rising from the earth below*.]

ERDA: Wotan... give up the Ring! It is the only way to avoid Alberich's curse. If you do not... all the Gods are doomed!

[*Exit* ERDA, *returning back into the earth*.]

WOTAN: [*Placing the Ring on the pile*] Freia, you are free. Bring us our youth once more.

[FREIA *goes free. She rushes into the arms of* FRICKA, DONNER *and* FROH. *The Giants cross to the pile of Gold.* FASOLT *takes the Ring and puts it on his finger.* FAFNER *takes the Tarnhelm and the Gold*.]

FAFNER: [*Envying the Ring on* FASOLT's *hand*] Brother... you take the Gold. Give me the Ring.

FASOLT: No! You take the Gold and *I'll* have the Ring.

[FASOLT *and* FAFNER *(improvising lines) continue to fight over the spoils. Whereupon* FAFNER *kills* FASOLT *with a blow of his sword, and tears the Ring from his dead brother's grasp. All are horrified. Exit* FAFNER *dragging off the body of* FASOLT, *leaving his sword behind.*]

WOTAN: [*With disdain*] See the curse's power!

[WOTAN *crosses downstage, picks up the sword and looks off in the direction of the Giants.* FRICKA *crosses to* WOTAN.]

FRICKA: [*Caressing and coaxing him*] Come, Wotan, let's go home to our castle.

WOTAN: Donner, clear the mist that hides my castle.

[*Blackout. Cue: Lightning and Thunder.*]

DONNER: [*Not seen through the storm*] Vapors! Fog! Mist, away! To my hammer's swing away! Brother, show them the way to the bridge.

[*Lights up as Lightning and Thunder subside. A rainbow bridge is clearly visible leading to the castle, Valhalla, glimmering in the distance as before.* DONNER *and* FROH *stand on either side of the bridge's entrance.*]

FROH: This bridge leads you homeward. Light, yet firm to your feet. Tread undaunted in its terrorless path!

[WOTAN, *holding both his spear and* FAFNER'S *sword, points the sword toward the castle. Music cue 7.*]

WOTAN: Come to Valhalla, the home of the Gods!

[*All, in turn, process over the rainbow bridge to the castle, except* LOGE. *He remains alone and looks down at the Rhine. The River flows but the* RHINEMAIDENS *no longer swim happily about. They are sad to have lost the Gold.* LOGE *turns and looks up at the castle and disparagingly anticipates the Gods' downfall. Then, assuming a careless manner,* LOGE *crosses over the rainbow bridge to join the other Gods in Valhalla.*]

CURTAIN
THE END of *DAS RHEINGOLD*

DIE WALKÜRE

The Valkyrie

CHARACTERS

SIEGLINDE
SIEGMUND
HUNDING
WOTAN
BRÜNNHILDE, *a Valkyrie*
FRICKA
VALKYRIES, *Warrior Maidens*

ACT I: Hunding's Dwelling, in the Forest
ACT II: A Rocky Pass
ACT III: The Valkyries' Rock

ACT I
Hunding's Dwelling, in the Forest

[*Music cue 1. Curtain.*]

An enormous ash tree fills the stage. From the trunk of the tree stems a gold sword (it is the sword left behind by FAFNER *at the end of Das Rheingold). A storm is subsiding. Lightning continues for a time.*

[*Enter* SIEGMUND, *exhausted from running. He collapses on the floor. Music fades. Enter* SIEGLINDE, *carrying a drinking horn. She expects the sound to be her husband returning home.*]

SIEGLINDE: [*As she enters*] Hunding...Hunding, is that you? [*seeing* SIEGMUND] No, it isn't. Who is this stranger?
[*She tries to rouse him. He wakes.*]
SIEGMUND: Water.... Water.... Please, something to drink.
[*She gives him water. Music cue 2.*]
SIEGMUND: [*As he revives*] Who are you? Where am I?
SIEGLINDE: I am Sieglinde. I am the wife of Hunding. This is his house. Why were you out wandering in this terrible storm?
SIEGMUND: I was in combat with an enemy tribe. My sword and shield were destroyed and I had to run for my life. [*He begins to leave.*] Thank you for your kindness.
SIEGLINDE: Please, rest a while.
SIEGMUND: [*Stopping*] No, I must be on my way. Wherever

31

I go bad luck follows with me. My bad fortune should not come to your house.

SIEGLINDE: Trouble cannot be brought to a place where bad luck already dwells.

[*Music cue 3. Enter* HUNDING.]

HUNDING: [*As he enters*] Sieglinde! Sieglinde! Is my supper ready? [*Seeing* SIEGMUND] Sieglinde...who is this stranger?

SIEGLINDE: He is a traveler who came to our house during the storm. I gave him something to drink.

HUNDING: You must be very tired. Stay and share our meal.

SIEGMUND: Thank you.

HUNDING: [*Noticing the resemblance of* SIEGMUND *and* SIEGLINDE] It is strange how much alike you and my wife look. Who are you? Where are you from?

SIEGMUND: I am called "Woeful" of the tribe of "Walsungs." We all used to live happily in the forest: my father, my mother and my twin sister. One day my father came home and found our house burned to the ground and my mother murdered. There was no sign of my sister. The *evil* tribe that did this were the Neidungs!

HUNDING: Woeful! I am a Neidung! You are an enemy under my roof! Stay the night but prepare to defend yourself in the morning. Sieglinde, prepare my evening drink!

[*Exit* HUNDING *followed by* SIEGLINDE.]

SIEGMUND: [*Not having noticed the sword in the tree*] What will I do? I am alone in the house of an enemy. Where is the sword my father promised that I would find in my hour of need?

[*Music cue 4. Light beams in on the Gold Sword. Enter* SIEGLINDE.]

SIEGLINDE: Woeful, are you listening? Hunding will not hear us. I have mixed a sleeping potion in his drink.

SIEGMUND: What are you saying?

SIEGLINDE: I didn't want to marry Hunding, I was forced to. During the wedding feast a man came to the house and thrust this sword into the tree. [*Pointing to the sword*] He said, the sword belonged to the warrior who one day

would pull it free. Many have tried but all have failed.
I believe you are the one to claim the sword and rescue
me from my terrible life.

SIEGMUND: [*With excitement*] Sieglinde, it was my father
who left the sword there. I am destined to have it. Could
it be that *you* are my long lost *sister?*

SIEGLINDE: Yes, we are the children of the stranger with the
sword. Your name should no longer be "Woeful" but
"Siegmund," just as mine is Sieglinde!

[SIEGLINDE *leads* SIEGMUND *to the tree to pull out the
sword.*]

SIEGMUND: [*With powerful effort, as he pulls the sword*]
Needful! Needful! Needful!

[*Music cue* 5. SIEGMUND *releases the sword and holds
it triumphantly above his head.* SIEGLINDE *screams in
amazement. They rush to each others arms and flee into
the night, sword in hand.*]

CURTAIN

ACT II
A Rocky Pass

[*Music cue* 6. *Curtain.*]

At rise, WOTAN *and* BRÜNNHILDE *are in full armor. Music fades.*

WOTAN: Brünnhilde, call your sisters, the Valkyries. Ride to the aid of Siegmund. Soon he will have to face Hunding in battle. He will need our help.
  [BRÜNNHILDE *climbs to a rocky ledge and calls the* VALKYRIES *with her battle cry. Music cue* 7.]

BRÜNNHILDE: [*Mouths to a recording*]
  Hojotoho! Hojotoho!
  Heiaha! Heiaha!
  Hojotoho! Hojotoho!
  Heiaha! Heiaha!
  Hojotoho! Hojotoho!
  Hojotoho! Hojotoho!
  Heiahaha! Hojoho!
  [*Music fades.* BRÜNNHILDE *looks in the distance and sees* FRICKA *approaching, then crosses to* WOTAN.]

BRÜNNHILDE: Father, I see Fricka. She seems to be coming this way.

WOTAN: I wonder what she is going to complain about now. Thank you, Brünnhilde. Continue to call the Valkyries.
  [*Enter* FRICKA.]

FRICKA: Wotan, I am furious! How could you dare permit Siegmund to steal away with Hunding's wife? As the Goddess of Marriage, it is my duty to see that marriage vows are kept. I demand that you punish the two guilty lovers!

WOTAN: Fricka, I cannot. We are in need of a mortal champion. There are things we Gods cannot do ourselves. I have destined Siegmund. But, he must have my protection.

FRICKA: What you are doing is wrong. Siegmund stole Hunding's wife. He is a sinful mortal. You must promise to doom Siegmund!

[FRICKA *leaves* WOTAN. *He sits on a ledge down right. She crosses to* BRÜNNHILDE.] [*Snidely*] Oh, Brünnhilde, I've just had a talk with your father. I believe I've made him see what a mess he has caused with Siegmund and Sieglinde running off together.

[*Exit* FRICKA. BRÜNNHILDE *crosses to* WOTAN.]

WOTAN: [*Upset over his argument with* FRICKA] Daughter, when Alberich stole the Gold from the Rhinemaidens all our power vanished. I have tried and tried to get back the Ring. Siegmund was to be our salvation. I gave him a magic sword in hopes that he would recover it. But now the Ring's curse will strike again because Fricka has forced me to deny Siegmund protection in battle with Hunding. All our power and glory are gone!

BRÜNNHILDE: Oh, father, what are we to do?

WOTAN: [*Standing*] There remains only a dismal end. Alberich has bought a woman with the Gold. She will give him a son who will continue his evil work. Here I am, a God, and I can find no one to save the world. Brünnhilde, Siegmund must die.

BRÜNNHILDE: No, father, no! Please save Siegmund!

WOTAN: [*Bitterly*] I wish it were not so. Siegmund is my mortal son. You must obey my orders.

[*Exit* WOTAN. *Music cue 8.* BRÜNNHILDE *crosses to the higher ground and observes as* SIEGMUND *and* SIEGLINDE *enter the Rocky Pass. Enter* SIEGMUND *and* SIEGLINDE. *Her dress is torn and spattered with mud. Music fades.*]

SIEGLINDE: Please, Siegmund, leave me.

SIEGMUND: No, Sieglinde. We must hurry.

SIEGLINDE: Let me die here alone in shame.

[SIEGLINDE, *exhausted, faints in* SIEGMUND's *arms.*
BRÜNNHILDE *crosses toward the front and stands looking
gravely down at* SIEGMUND *and* SIEGLINDE.]

SIEGMUND: [*Looking up and seeing* BRÜNNHILDE] Who are
you?

BRÜNNHILDE: Only heros about to die in battle may gaze
upon me. I have come to take you to Valhalla to join the
other heroes.

SIEGMUND: Wait, let me get Sieglinde.

BRÜNNHILDE: No, Siegmund, you must part from her forever.

SIEGMUND: No! I will remain and defend the two of us with
my magic sword.

BRÜNNHILDE: The sword's magic has been taken away. You
will be killed by Hunding.

SIEGMUND: [*Drawing his sword*] Then I will kill Sieglinde
and myself rather than part from her.

BRÜNNHILDE: [*Aside, overcome with sympathy*] Now what
would you do? What would Wotan do if he were here?
They seem to be so much in love. [*To* SIEGMUND] All
right, I'll help you. The sword will serve you in battle.
I will be there with you to change the outcome.

[*Enter* HUNDING.]

HUNDING: Woeful! Prepare to die in battle!

[HUNDING *and* SIEGMUND *battle, for a time, shielded by*
BRÜNNHILDE. *Enter* WOTAN. BRÜNNHILDE *in the presence
of* WOTAN, *recoils in terror.* WOTAN *breaks* SIEGMUND's
sword with a blow of his spear. Music cue 9. HUNDING
thrusts his sword into SIEGMUND, *killing him.* BRÜNNHILDE
picks up the shattered pieces of SIEGMUND's *sword then
rushes to* SIEGLINDE *and the two hurry away. With a
gesture of his hand,* WOTAN *kills* HUNDING.]

WOTAN: [*With a terrible anger*] Brünnhilde, you will regret
this crime. You will be punished for disobeying me!
[*Blackout.*]

CURTAIN

ACT III
The Valkyries' Rock

[*Music cue* 10. *Curtain.*]

The VALKYRIES *assemble and wait for the return of* BRÜNN-HILDE. *Music fades.*

[*Enter* BRÜNNHILDE *and* SIEGLINDE.]

A VALKYRIE: [*Alarmed*] Brünnhilde, what are you doing?

A VALKYRIE: This is a place for lost heroes.

A VALKYRIE: Why have you brought a woman here?

A VALKYRIE: We are expecting you to bring Siegmund.

BRÜNNHILDE: This is Sieglinde. She and Siegmund were running from Hunding when he caught up with them. Father told me that Hunding should kill Siegmund in battle. But I tried to rearrange things and was caught. Father saw that Siegmund was killed and I came here with Sieglinde.

A VALKYRIE: Where is father now?

BRÜNNHILDE: On his way to punish me for what I did. Can any of you help us to escape?

VALKYRIES: No, Brünnhilde.... We can not.... Father would be angry with us.... *(etc.)*

BRÜNNHILDE: [*Urgently*] Sisters, please save us! Father is so angry with me.

A VALKYRIE: Go eastward to the cave in the forest where Fafner sleeps on the Gold.

A VALKYRIE: Yes, there you will be safe.

A VALKYRIE: Wotan will never find you.

[BRÜNNHILDE *and* SIEGLINDE *cross to the other side of the stage.*]

BRÜNNHILDE: Sieglinde, have courage. You are soon to bear a son. He will be the world's most glorious hero: Siegfried. [BRÜNNHILDE *hands* SIEGLINDE *the broken pieces of* SIEGMUND'*s sword.*] Here are the fragments of Siegmund's sword.

[SIEGLINDE *and the* VALKYRIES *wave good-bye to one another. Exit* SIEGLINDE. *Enter* WOTAN.]

WOTAN: Brünnhilde, come forth!

VALKYRIES: Oh, father.... Please be merciful.... *(etc.)*

WOTAN: Brünnhilde, for deliberately disobeying me, you shall henceforth no longer be a Valkyrie. [*To the other* VALKYRIES] Have nothing more to do with your sister. If you do, the same punishment will be yours!

[*Exit* VALKYRIES.]

BRÜNNHILDE: [*Humbly*] Father, I did not mean to disobey you. I was so touched by Siegmund's love for Sieglinde. I only did what you originally wanted.

WOTAN: You aroused my anger and must be punished. I will put you to sleep on this mountaintop. Here you will remain until a man comes and takes you as his bride.

BRÜNNHILDE: Father, I will obey. But asleep, unprotected, I would be easy prey to the basest coward. Shield me with terrors, that a hero alone may find me. Surround me with a wall of fire until the hero comes.

[*Music cue* 11. WOTAN *leads* BRÜNNHILDE *up the mountaintop. Taking her spear and shield,* WOTAN *kisses* BRÜNNHILDE'*s forehead.*]

WOTAN: Thus the God takes away your Godhood! [WOTAN *walks* BRÜNNHILDE *to the mountain peak where she lies down for her long sleep.* WOTAN *covers her with her shield and lays her spear beside her.* WOTAN *strikes his spear three times and fire encircles the mountaintop.* WOTAN *descends the mountain, passes through the wall of fire, stops, turns and sees his daughter engulfed in flames.*] Only the man who does not fear my spear may walk through this fire.

[WOTAN *turns and looks at* BRÜNNHILDE *one last time and slowly exits.*]

CURTAIN
THE END of *DIE WALKÜRE*

SIEGFRIED

CHARACTERS

MIME
SIEGFRIED, *son of Siegmund and Sieglinde*
WOTAN, *disguised as* the Wanderer
ALBERICH
FAFNER, *transformed into a dragon*
FOREST BIRD
ERDA
BRÜNNHILDE, *formerly a Valkyrie, now a mortal*

ACT I
Mime's Cave

[*Music cue 1. Curtain.*]

To one side of the stage is an anvil. MIME *is at work forging a sword for* SIEGFRIED *(who he has raised since birth). He hammers in time to the music. Music fades.*

MIME: [*Pausing from his work*] I'm so disgusted! Every time I make a sword for Siegfried he goes and breaks it. That is just what he will do with this one. If only I could repair the sword "Needful" all my troubles would be over. With that sword, I could have Siegfried kill Fafner and recover the Rhine Gold. Then *I* could have the Ring and it would be *my* turn to rule the world.
[*Music cue 2. Enter* SIEGFRIED, *leading a bear.* * MIME *runs in terror.* SIEGFRIED *laughs. After the tease is over,* SIEGFRIED *chases the bear out.*]

SIEGFRIED: That bear is better company than you! [SIEGFRIED *crosses to the anvil and breaks the sword that* MIME *has been working on.*] You're so stupid. Why can't you make a sword that I can use?
[SIEGFRIED *sits and sulks.* MIME *brings him a bowl of food.* SIEGFRIED *knocks the bowl from* MIME's *hands.*]

MIME: [*Annoyed*] Siegfried, I have fathered you; I've fed

---

*NOTE: In production, the part of the bear may be ommitted. SIEGFRIED may enter, omit his first line and cross directly to break the sword.

47

you; clothed you; taught you all that I know. And for what? For ingratitude and abuse!

SIEGFRIED: [*Standing*] The only thing I've ever learned from you is that I don't like you. I don't know why I even bother to return home at all. The animals in the forest are far more friendly than you could ever be. At least they are all happy. The little ones look like their parents. You are the only parent I know . . . a whining little dwarf. I don't believe you are my father. Who are my *real* parents?

MIME: I don't know.

SIEGFRIED: [*Taking* MIME *by the throat*] I'll force you to tell me!

MIME: [*Overpowered*] All right . . . all right . . . I'll tell you. Many years ago, I found a woman helpless in the forest. She was about to have a baby so I took her to my cave. She gave birth, but then died. Before she died, she said that her name was Sieglinde and that the baby was to be named Siegfried.

SIEGFRIED: What about my father?

MIME: He was killed in combat.

SIEGFRIED: This is a very strange story. Where is your proof?

[MIME *produces the pieces of the broken sword, "Needful."*]

MIME: This broken sword was my only reward for my good deeds.

SIEGFRIED: I want these pieces to be put back together to make my new sword. And if you don't do it, I'm going to give you the worst beating.

[*Exit* SIEGFRIED.]

MIME: [*Alone*] What will I do? I haven't the skill to fix this sword.

[MIME *returns to the anvil to continue his work. Enter* WOTAN *disguised as* the WANDERER.]

WANDERER: Excuse me, sir, may I come and rest? I have been wandering for a long time.

[MIME *nods. The* WANDERER *sits on a ledge up left.*] I

have been wandering all over the world and I have learned a great deal. I have discovered that man is lacking in wisdom.

MIME: I am content with the wisdom I already have.

WANDERER: Ah...I'll tell you what, lets have a contest. My head if I lose.

MIME: All right. [*Aside*] I'll certainly trap this uninvited guest. [*To* the WANDERER] First, who are the people who live in the depths of the earth?

WANDERER: The Nibelungs. Alberich is their ruler. He had lost the magic Gold. With it he had planned to rule the world.

MIME: Who rules the surface of the earth?

WANDERER: The Giants, Fasolt and Fafner, *used* to rule there. They were given Alberich's Gold but quarreled and Fafner killed Fasolt. Fafner has now made himself become a dragon and guards the treasure.

MIME: Who rules the skies?

[*Music cue* 3.]

WANDERER: [*Over music*] The Gods rule above. Wotan is their Monarch. With his spear he rules over Gods, Nibelungs and Giants alike. [*Music fades*.] Now it is your turn. To whom is Wotan most severe but loves above all others?

MIME: The Walsungs. The best-loved were Siegmund and Sieglinde and their son, Siegfried.

WANDERER: With what sword will Siegfried have to slay the dragon Fafner and recover the Gold?

MIME: The sword known as "Needful."

WANDERER: Who will mend the broken sword?

MIME: [*Terrified*] I don't know! I don't know!

WANDERER: [*Standing to warn him*] Only he who knows no fear can mend the sword. Don't worry, I will save your head for the fearless one.

[*Exit the* WANDERER. *Enter* SIEGFRIED.]

SIEGFRIED: Well, is my sword ready?

MIME: No, Siegfried. I've been too concerned with fears for your sake to work on it.

SIEGFRIED: Fear . . . what is fear?

MIME: I will take you to the dragon's cave. There you will learn this lesson.

SIEGFRIED: I want you to fix that sword!

MIME: It's too hard for me.

SIEGFRIED: Then I'll do it myself. [SIEGFRIED *pushes* MIME *out of his way and crosses to the anvil.*]

[*Music cue* 4. MIME *watches in amazement as* SIEGFRIED *hammers the sword. When the sword is finished,* SIEGFRIED *holds it triumphantly above his head. Then, laughing joyously,* SIEGFRIED *rushes off into the forest.*]

CURTAIN

ACT II
Deep in the Forest

[*Music cue 5. Curtain.*]

At rise, ALBERICH, *hoping to recover the magic Gold, waits outside the mouth of* FAFNER'*s cave up left. To the right are trees which cover the higher ground.*

[*Enter* the WANDERER. *Music fades.*]

ALBERICH: [*Recognizing* the WANDERER *to be* WOTAN *in disguise*] What are you doing here? You always want to cause me trouble.

WANDERER: At this very minute Mime is on his way to Fafner's cave. He is with a youth who knows no fear. He will get back the Ring. Tell Fafner to give up the Ring.

ALBERICH: [*Calling into* FAFNER'*s cave*] Fafner, I think you should give up the Ring. Keep the Gold if you want to, but give up the Ring.

FAFNER: [*From within*] (GROWL!) The Ring is mine!

[*Exit the* WANDERER, *laughing.*]

ALBERICH: I'll have my revenge!

[*Exit* ALBERICH. *Enter* SIEGFRIED *and* MIME.]

SIEGFRIED: Well, when are you going to teach me this lesson?

MIME: Inside this cave is a dragon. His breath is poison. His saliva will corrode bones and flesh. Soon he will feel your sword in his heart.

SIEGFRIED: All this is nonsense in place of my lesson. Go for a walk and leave me alone.

[*Exit* MIME. *Music cue* 6.]

[SIEGFRIED *sits under the trees and eats his lunch. Enter* FAFNER, *from the cave. He wears the Ring. Music fades.*]

FAFNER: Who dares disturb my sleep?

SIEGFRIED: [*Standing up*] Are you going to teach me fear?

[FAFNER *bellows with rage.* SIEGFRIED *draws his sword and drives it into* FAFNER's *heart. Wounded,* FAFNER *falls to the ground.*]

FAFNER: [*Dying*] Who sent you here to kill me?

SIEGFRIED: I killed you in self-defense.

FAFNER: [*Growing weaker*] It is Alberich's curse that has killed me. He plans your death, too.

SIEGFRIED: Do you know who I am?

FAFNER: Siegfried . . . Siegfried . . . [*He dies.*]

[SIEGFRIED *takes the Ring from* FAFNER *and puts it on his hand. He then tastes the blood on his sword which enables him to understand the language of* the FOREST BIRD.]

[*Enter* the FOREST BIRD, *in flight.*]

FOREST BIRD: Siegfried, the Gold is inside Fafner's cave.

[*Exit* SIEGFRIED *following* the FOREST BIRD *into the cave. Enter* ALBERICH *and* MIME, *who carries a draught of poison brew.*]

ALBERICH: Now *I* can have the Gold!

MIME: And we could split the treasure?

ALBERICH: No we won't! Do you think I would let you have any of it?

MIME: Maybe just the Tarnhelm?

ALBERICH: No!

[*Exit* ALBERICH. *Enter* SIEGFRIED *and* the FOREST BIRD. SIEGFRIED *wears the Ring and carries the Tarnhelm which he examines and then tucks under his belt.*]

FOREST BIRD: Siegfried, the taste of Fafner's blood has not only made you able to understand the language of the animals in the forest, but the real meaning behind Mime's deceitful words. Beware, Siegfried, Mime plans to trick you!

[MIME *crosses to* SIEGFRIED *carrying the poison draught.*]

MIME: [*In a manner flattering* SIEGFRIED] Come, Siegfried, have something to drink.

SIEGFRIED: [*Aside*] What he means is, let me poison you, chop off your head and take the Ring. [*To* MIME] You are going to poison me, aren't you?

MIME: [*Astonished*] No, Siegfried, please have something to drink. [MIME *holds the draught out to* SIEGFRIED. SIEGFRIED *raises his sword and kills* MIME *with one blow.* ALBERICH's *laughter is heard from off stage.*]

FOREST BIRD: Siegfried, asleep on top of a great mountain ringed in flames, is Brünnhilde. It is only a man who has never known fear who can pass through these flames and win Brünnhilde as his bride.

SIEGFRIED: I am that hero! Please, lead me to Brünnhilde's rock!

[*Music cue* 7. *Exit* SIEGFRIED, *holding his sword aloft, following the path of* the FOREST BIRD.]

CURTAIN

ACT III
Scene 1: The Foot of the Mountain

[*Music cue 8. Curtain.*]

A storm is raging. The WANDERER *paces amid the lightning and thunder. He calls out for* ERDA, *the Earth Goddess.*

WANDERER: Erda! Erda! [*Music fades. Enter* ERDA, *rising from the earth below.*] Erda, how can we stop this awful process of fate? Everyone who possesses the Ring is doomed to die. What is the point of having the power of the Ring if you know that you soon will die?

ERDA: Wotan . . . ask your daughter, Brünnhilde. She, too, is endowed with godlike wisdom.

WANDERER: I can't ask Brünnhilde. I put her to sleep years ago and built a ring of fire around her.

ERDA: Wotan . . . what a stupid thing to do! With all the sins on your conscience, you are hardly in the position to punish anyone so severely.

WANDERER: Erda, years ago you gave to me wisdom. That wisdom has only made me confused. Now, I must resign myself that the Gods will be destroyed. But Siegfried has won the Ring! He is full of youth and love. He will win Brünnhilde and redeem the world. Erda, you have been no help at all. Go back to sleep!

[*Exit* ERDA, *back into the earth. Enter* the FOREST BIRD *followed by* SIEGFRIED. *The* FOREST BIRD, *recognizing the* WANDERER *to be* WOTAN *in disguise, becomes frightened and flies away.*]

SIEGFRIED: [*Coming upon* the WANDERER] Excuse me, sir.

Could you tell me the way to the fire-encircled rock?

WANDERER: Tell me, where did you get that sword?

SIEGFRIED: From Mime, he had the pieces of it. It had been broken.

WANDERER: Who repaired it?

SIEGFRIED: I did.

WANDERER: Who made the sword in the first place?

SIEGFRIED: I don't know. But it was of no use to anyone all broken.

WANDERER: That is obvious. [*He laughs.*]

SIEGFRIED: Well, I don't have any more time to stand around and talk. I must be on my way.

WANDERER: [*Pointing to the rocky heights*] Look up to the mountain where the great fire is seen. There the maiden slumbers. But, he who dares go near that spot will be consumed in flames. [SIEGFRIED *tries to get past. The* WANDERER *bars* SIEGFRIED's *way with his spear.*] This spear once shattered the very sword you hold in your hand.

SIEGFRIED: [*Drawing his sword*] At last, my father's enemy! [SIEGFRIED *breaks* the WANDERER's *spear into two pieces, with a single blow of his sword. Lightning flashes. Black out. Music cue 9.*]

END OF SCENE 1*

Scene 2: The Valkyrie Rock

Fire surrounds the mountaintop. BRÜNNHILDE *sleeps (as in Die Walküre, Act III) covered by her shield.*

[*Enter* SIEGFRIED, *his sword aloft. As* SIEGFRIED *passes*

---

*NOTE: There should be no curtain between Scenes 1 and 2.

through the flames and climbs the mountaintop he sees
a reclining warrior. Music fades.]

SIEGFRIED: Who is this? [*Coming closer*] It is a man ... in
armor. He can't be very comfortable under that heavy
shield. [SIEGFRIED *removes the shield and is astonished*
to see that the warrior is a woman.] This is no man!

[SIEGFRIED *bends down and gently kisses* BRÜNNHILDE.
She awakens.]

BRÜNNHILDE: Who has awakened me from my long sleep?

SIEGFRIED: I am Siegfried.

BRÜNNHILDE: Siegfried ... Siegfried ... hero! You are the
son of Sieglinde, whom I befriended in defiance of Wotan.
As punishment for my crime, I have been prisoner on
this mountaintop. It was all for the love of you.

SIEGFRIED: [*Aside, tenderly*] I feel this strange emotion.
Could this be fear?

BRÜNNHILDE: [*Seeing her armor*] Here is my shield.
[BRÜNNHILDE *remembers that* WOTAN *has taken her God-*
hood away.] Oh, the disgrace! My Godhood has been
taken away! I am no longer a Valkyrie! I am no longer
Brünnhilde!

SIEGFRIED: [*With great emotion*] You are to me!

[SIEGFRIED *tries to embrace* BRÜNNHILDE. *She shyly es-*
capes his advance.]

BRÜNNHILDE: [*With much sadness*] I am confused. Oh, Siegfried, pity me and leave me in peace.

SIEGFRIED: I love you, Brünnhilde. Didn't you just say that
you loved me? I want you to be my bride!

BRÜNNHILDE: [*With deep feeling*] Oh, Siegfried, I will follow you to my doom. [*Music cue* 10. BRÜNNHILDE *opens*
her arms to the heavens.] Good-bye Valhalla and to the
splendor of the Gods!

[BRÜNNHILDE *turns, arms now outstretched to* SIEG-
FRIED. SIEGFRIED *then opens his arms to* BRÜNNHILDE.
Slowly they cross into each other's arms.]

CURTAIN
THE END of *SIEGFRIED*

GÖTTERDÄMMERUNG

(Twilight of the Gods)

CHARACTERS

BRÜNNHILDE
SIEGFRIED
HAGAN, *Son of Alberich*
GUNTHER
GUTRUNE
WALTRAUTE, *a Valkyrie*
ALBERICH
THREE RHINEMAIDENS
VASSALS
LADIES
HUNTERS

PROLOGUE*:		The Valkyries' Rock
ACT I:	Scene 1:	The Gibichung's Hall
	Scene 2:	The Valkyries' Rock
ACT II:		The Gibichung's Hall
ACT III:	Scene 1:	A Forest Clearing by the Rhine
	Scene 2:	The Castle Giblich

*NOTE: In the original operatic version of Wagner's Ring Cycle, the Prologue to *Götterdämmerung* begins with a lengthy scene featuring the Three Norns or "Fates." In the interest of time, as *The Ring* is intended to be performed in one evening, I have chosen to omit this part of the story.

PROLOGUE
The Valkyries' Rock

[*Music cue 1. Curtain.*]

It is dawn. Morning light fills the mountaintop.

[*Enter* BRÜNNHILDE *and* SIEGFRIED *from a cave. Music fades.*]

BRÜNNHILDE: Now, Siegfried, you must go and do glorious deeds. I confess...that I have one misgiving.

SIEGFRIED: What Brünnhilde?

BRÜNNHILDE: I am troubled about sending you away.

SIEGFRIED: Why?

BRÜNNHILDE: I have given you wisdom at the cost of my Godhood. Now I have only mortal love left for you. One day as a man, you might reject my love. Siegfried, my hero, never forget our pledges of love.

SIEGFRIED: Brünnhilde, don't worry, I never will. I promise to go and do glorious deeds and return back to you. As pledge of my good faith, here is the magic Ring.[*He gives her the Ring.*]

BRÜNNHILDE: [*Putting on the Ring in rapturous delight*] I will guard this with my life. In its place you must take my horse Grane.

SIEGFRIED: You alone give me courage! Our hearts beat as one!

BRÜNNHILDE: [*Holding her arms outstretched*] Oh, heavenly powers, see our love! Apart...who can divide us? Divided...we are still one!

SIEGFRIED: Hail, Brünnhilde!

BRÜNNHILDE: Hail, Siegfried!

[*Music cue 2.* SIEGFRIED *descends the mountaintop, crosses the stage, pauses and waves good-bye to* BRÜNNHILDE. *Exit* SIEGFRIED. BRÜNNHILDE, *alone on the mountaintop, watches and waves as the departing hero travels on his journey down the Rhine.*]

CURTAIN

ACT I

Scene 1: The Gibichung's Hall

[*Curtain.*]

Banners fill the hall. Upstage are two thrones where GUNTHER *and* GUTRUNE *are seated. Up right is a sailing vessel.* HAGEN *stands down stage. Music fades.*

HAGEN: Gunther, neither you nor your sister, Gutrune, are married. I am very concerned over the future of our race, Gibich. I would suggest that you, Gunther, marry Brünnhilde. And for you, Gutrune, Siegfried might make an excellent match. [HAGEN *crosses above the thrones and kneels between* GUNTHER *and* GUTRUNE.] Gunther, I have a plan. Today, Siegfried will travel down the Rhine. We will give him a potion that will not only put him in our power but will cause him to forget Brünnhilde and fall in love with Gutrune.
[*Music cue* 3. *Exit* GUTRUNE. *Enter* SIEGFRIED, *greeted by* HAGEN *and* GUNTHER.]

GUNTHER: Siegfried, welcome. My land, my vassals and I am at your service.

SIEGFRIED: Thank you. I can offer you nothing, but my strength and my sword.

HAGEN: We understand that you have won the magic Gold of the Nibelungen.

SIEGFRIED: Yes. The Gold was of no use to me though. All I kept was this mesh hat. [*Gesturing to the Tarnhelm*] I don't know what it is for.

HAGEN: It is the Tarnhelm. With it you can take on any shape you choose. Didn't you take anything else?

SIEGFRIED: Oh, yes, a ring. It is now on the hand of a woman.

HAGEN: [*Aside to* GUNTHER] Brünnhilde....

[*Enter* GUTRUNE *with a goblet containing the potion.*]

GUTRUNE: Siegfried, welcome to the Gibich's house. I've prepared you a drink. [*She hands* SIEGFRIED *the potion.*]

SIEGFRIED: [*Making a toast*] To Brünnhilde, my bride! [SIEGFRIED *drinks the potion. Its power takes over* SIEGFRIED'*s mind and body. He looks adoringly at* GUTRUNE.] [*Aside to* GUNTHER] Gunther, what is your sister's name?

GUNTHER: Gutrune.

SIEGFRIED: Gunther, have you a wife?

GUNTHER: No. The one I want lives on a far-off rock surrounded by fire. She is Brünnhilde.

SIEGFRIED: [*Not remembering* BRÜNNHILDE] On a far-off rock surrounded by fire....

GUNTHER: I cannot brave the fire to win her as my bride.

SIEGFRIED: I do not fear the fire. [*Aside*] I do not fear anything. [*To* GUNTHER] I will bring you your new wife if your sister Gutrune will be my bride. Yes, I will woo Brünnhilde for you. I will appear to be *you* with the use of the *Tarnhelm*.

GUNTHER: For that, Siegfried, Gutrune will be your bride. [GUNTHER *and* SIEGFRIED *prick their arms, join forearms and mix each other's blood.*]

GUNTHER and SIEGFRIED: To the oath of brotherhood!

GUNTHER: He who breaks the oath must pay with his heart's blood.

[GUNTHER *and* SIEGFRIED *cross upstage and board the boat. They unloosen the lug rigged sails and waving to* GUTRUNE, *sail off.*]

GUTRUNE: [*Looking off toward the boat, waving*] Oh... Siegfried!

[*Music cue* 4.]

HAGEN: [*Aside*] I hope the search for Gunther's bride brings *me* back the Ring!

CURTAIN

Scene 2: The Valkyrie Rock

[*Curtain.*]

At rise, BRÜNNHILDE, *alone on the mountaintop, contemplates* SIEGFRIED *and the Ring. Lightning flashes from offstage.* BRÜNNHILDE *looks off into the distance. Music fades.*

BRÜNNHILDE: Who is this I see coming in the distance? It is my sister, Waltraute. [*Enter* WALTRAUTE.] Waltraute, why all the excitement? I know, you have come to tell me that Wotan has finally forgiven me. You see, Wotan's punishment was a blessing in disguise. It brought me Siegfried. It brought me love.

WALTRAUTE: Wotan is awaiting the Gods' downfall. But, all this can be stopped if you return the Ring back to the Rhinemaidens. Alberich's curse will be broken and the peace of Valhalla is assured. Please, Brünnhilde, give up the Ring!

BRÜNNHILDE: I will never part with the token of Siegfried's love, even if it does mean the Gods' destruction!

WALTRAUTE: Woe to the Gods of Valhalla!

[*Exit* WALTRAUTE. BRÜNNHILDE *crosses and looks off in the opposite direction, believing that she sees* SIEGFRIED *approaching.*]

BRÜNNHILDE: Look, here comes Siegfried! [*Enter* SIEG-

FRIED, *wearing the Tarnhelm, in the form of* GUNTHER.*]
Who are you? You are not Siegfried.

SIEGFRIED: [*In the form of* GUNTHER] I am Gunther. I have
come to take you as my bride!

BRÜNNHILDE: [*Holding forth the Ring*] Stand back! This
Ring is my shield!

[BRÜNNHILDE *and* SIEGFRIED, *in the form of* GUNTHER,
violently struggle. He tears the Ring from BRÜNNHILDE's
grasp. BRÜNNHILDE *screams loudly and sinks helpless
to the ground.*]

SIEGFRIED: [*In the form of* GUNTHER, *holding the Ring above
him*] Now you are mine, Gunther's bride!

[*Music cue 5.* SIEGFRIED, *in the form of* GUNTHER, *drags*
BRÜNNHILDE *into a cave. He then returns in his natural
form, still wearing the Tarnhelm, holding both his sword
and the Ring.*]

SIEGFRIED: [*In his natural form*] With this sword I guard
Gunther's bride!

[*Blackout.*]

CURTAIN

*NOTE: In production, the actor playing GUNTHER may play SIEG-
FRIED disguised as GUNTHER. Whereby, the actor playing SIEG-
FRIED may then enter from the cave and deliver the final line of
SIEGFRIED, in his natural form.

ACT II
The Gibichung's Hall

[Curtain.]

Banners fill the hall, as before. HAGEN, *leaning on his spear, awaits* SIEGFRIED'*s return.* ALBERICH *kneels before him.*

ALBERICH: Hagen, my son, it is very important that you get back the Ring before Brünnhilde returns it to the Rhine-maidens. Swear to me, your father, that you will regain the Ring.

HAGEN: Don't worry, I'll lay my hands on it all right. Then the might of the Gods will be ours!

[Exit ALBERICH. *Enter* SIEGFRIED, *unnoticed by* HAGEN, *still wearing the Tarnhelm.]*

SIEGFRIED: *[Tapping* HAGEN'*s shoulder from behind]* Hagen!

HAGEN: *[Surprised]* Siegfried!

SIEGFRIED: *[Removing the Tarnhelm and tucking it in his belt]* The Tarnhelm transported me. Gunther and his bride are on their way.

[Enter GUTRUNE.]

GUTRUNE: Welcome home, Siegfried.

SIEGFRIED: *[Crossing to* GUTRUNE'*s side]* This sword helped me not only to win Gunther's bride, but a bride for me as well.

GUTRUNE: Hagen, call together the wedding procession.

HAGEN: Vassals! Vassals! *[Enter* VASSALS *from all directions.]* Siegfried has won a Valkyrie as a bride for Gunther! He himself will wed Gutrune! You are all invited to the wedding!

VASSALS: [*Cheering*] Hail! Hail! Hail!

[*Enter* GUNTHER *and* BRÜNNHILDE *by boat.* GUNTHER *ties up the sails and steps out of the boat leading* BRÜNNHILDE, *who follows him with lowered eyes.*]

GUNTHER: I have brought Brünnhilde, my bride, home to the Rhine. No man ever won a more noble woman!

VASSALS: [*Cheering*] Hail! Hail! Hail!

[GUNTHER *leads* BRÜNNHILDE *forward to greet the others. She slowly looks up and sees the Ring on* SIEGFRIED'*s hand.*]

GUNTHER: [*To* SIEGFRIED] Hero, I greet you. [*To* GUTRUNE] And to you sister. To the two happy couples: Gunther and Brünnhilde, Siegfried and Gutrune!

BRÜNNHILDE: [*Pointing to the Ring with terror and vehemence*] (SCREAM!) The Ring is on Siegfried's hand! Siegfried, you are my husband, not Gunther! Gunther stole the Ring from my hand! Why is it now on Siegfried's hand?

GUNTHER: [*Perplexed*] Wait, I didn't give the Ring to Siegfried.

BRÜNNHILDE: [*To* SIEGFRIED, *furiously*] Then it was you! You betrayed me and stole the Ring!

SIEGFRIED: [*Calm, still under the potion*] No, I stole the Ring from a dragon, not from a woman.

HAGEN: Yes, Siegfried, it *was* you! I demand vengeance on my brother Gunther's good name.

SIEGFRIED: I don't understand, my sword guards my trust.

HAGEN: [*Holding forward his spear*] Hold my spear and swear, Siegfried.

SIEGFRIED: [*Holding* HAGEN'*s spear*] I swear that I was never married to Brünnhilde.

BRÜNNHILDE: [*Furiously grasping* HAGEN'*s spear*] May this spear cause the destruction of Siegfried for his betrayal!

SIEGFRIED: [*To* GUNTHER, *unconcerned*] Gunther, give the women time to rest. [*To all*] Now come everyone, to the wedding party.

[*Exit* SIEGFRIED, GUTRUNE *and* VASSALS.]

HAGEN: Brünnhilde, we will help you revenge Siegfried. How can the hero's death be possible?

BRÜNNHILDE: Siegfried cannot be beaten in battle, unless he is attacked from behind. He is vulnerable there because the Gods never thought he would turn his back on a foe.

HAGEN: Then his back will be the target for my spear!

GUNTHER: [*Apprehensively*] Siegfried...dead? Now I'm not sure I want to be involved. Gutrune might get very upset.

HAGEN: [*Aside to* GUNTHER] The death of Siegfried will give us the Ring. Gutrune won't find out. Tomorrow we will all go on a hunt. We can say that Siegfried was killed by a wild boar.

[BRÜNNHILDE *and* GUNTHER *clasp their hands on* HAGEN's *spear.*]

BRÜNNHILDE, GUNTHER *and* HAGEN: For Siegfried's lie we swear revenge!

[*Music cue* 6. *Enter* SIEGFRIED *and* GUTRUNE *followed by the* VASSALS *forming the wedding procession.*]

HAGEN: [*Aside, as he watches the procession pass*] Alberich and I will be the Ring's new Lord!

[*As the procession passes below,* HAGEN *crosses to* GUNTHER *and* BRÜNNHILDE *and leads them to join the procession.*]

CURTAIN

ACT III

Scene 1: A Forest Clearing, by the Rhine.

[*Music cue 7. Curtain.*]

Blue-green light reveals the Rhine which flows below. The
RHINEMAIDENS *swim near the surface.*

> [*Enter* SIEGFRIED, *above on the higher ground. He lays
> down his shield and crosses down toward the bank of the
> Rhine to talk to the* RHINEMAIDENS.]

SIEGFRIED: [*Over music*] Excuse me. Have any of you ladies
    seen the animal I've been chasing?
RHINEMAIDEN I: If we tell you, will you give us the Ring?
SIEGFRIED: No, I won't!
RHINEMAIDEN II: You're cheap!
RHINEMAIDEN III: Why won't you give us the Ring?
SIEGFRIED: I'm going to keep it myself.
RHINEMAIDEN I: Beware Siegfried. The Ring's curse will
    strike you down today.
SIEGFRIED: Don't be silly. I'm a hero. I don't even know
    the meaning of fear.
RHINEMAIDEN II: Beware Siegfried. Death before nightfall.
RHINEMAIDEN III: Siegfried, the curse falls on the owner of
    the Ring!
> [SIEGFRIED *laughs. The Rhine River and the* RHINEMAID-
> ENS *fade out of view.* SIEGFRIED *crosses to the higher
> ground. Music fades. Enter* HAGEN *and* GUNTHER, *fol-
> lowed by* HUNTERS.]
SIEGFRIED: [*Greeting* HAGEN *and* GUNTHER] Friends, I've

73

lost track of the animal I've been chasing. I was wandering here along the Rhine and three mermaids told me that I was going to be killed before nightfall.

GUNTHER: [*Aside to* HAGEN] I'm scared, Hagen.

HAGEN: [*Aside to* GUNTHER] Don't worry. This will bring back his memory. [HAGEN *hands* SIEGFRIED *a drinking horn containing a potion that will restore his memory.* SIEGFRIED *drinks the potion.*] Siegfried, tell us about your past.

SIEGFRIED: [*His memory coming back*] Not long ago I climbed to the top of a burning mountain. There I passed through the flames to find a sleeping woman. She is Brünnhilde, my bride.

HAGEN: [*Pointing at two ravens*] Look, Siegfried, at the two ravens flying toward the Rhine.

[SIEGFRIED *turns to look at the ravens whereupon* HAGEN *thrusts his spear into* SIEGFRIED's *back. Wounded,* SIEGFRIED *falls to the ground.*]

SIEGFRIED: [*Reaching out in great pain*] Brünnhilde . . . Brünnhilde . . . [*He dies.*]

[HUNTERS *crowd around the body of* SIEGFRIED.]

HUNTERS: [*Astonished*] Hagen, what have you done?

HAGEN: I have avenged the lie!

[*Music cue* 8. *The* HUNTERS *place* SIEGFRIED's *body on his shield and carry the hero in a solemn procession over the higher ground.* HAGEN *and* GUNTHER *follow. Lights fade.*]

CURTAIN

Scene 2: The Castle Gibich

[*Curtain.*]

It is night. GUTRUNE *paces and waits for* SIEGFRIED *to return with the hunting party. Music fades.*

[*Enter* HAGEN *and* GUNTHER, *followed by the* HUNTERS *carrying the dead body of* SIEGFRIED. HAGEN *crosses directly to* GUTRUNE. *The* HUNTERS *place* SIEGFRIED'*s body slightly right of center and exit.*]

GUTRUNE: [*In great fear*] Hagen, what is it?

HAGEN: Siegfried was killed by a wild boar.

GUTRUNE: [*Rushing to* SIEGFRIED'*s corpse*] My husband!

GUNTHER: [*Trying to comfort her*] Gutrune...

GUTRUNE: [*Accusing* GUNTHER] It was you! It was you!

GUNTHER: [*Pointing to* HAGEN] No, it was him! Hagen is the guilty one!

HAGEN: [*Defiantly*] Yes, it was I who did it. Siegfried lied on the oath of my spear. The spear has now avenged its betrayer. The Ring is now mine by right.

GUNTHER: Now wait a minute. What do I get? And how about Gutrune, now she is a widow. I think we should get the Gold.

HAGEN: This is the Nibelungen's Gold! My father's treasure! [HAGEN *takes his spear and stabs* GUNTHER, *who falls wounded to the ground.*] Now...at last...the *Ring* is mine!

[HAGEN *grasps at the Ring on* SIEGFRIED'*s hand, which raises itself threateningly as a warning.* GUTRUNE *screams in terror. Enter* BRÜNNHILDE.]

BRÜNNHILDE: Silence! You are not fit for such a hero!

GUTRUNE: [*To* BRÜNNHILDE] *You* are the cause of all this trouble.

BRÜNNHILDE: *You* were *never* Siegfried's wife. You were a mere *interloper!*

GUTRUNE: We have all been victims of Hagen's treachery. I curse you Hagen!

[*Exit* GUTRUNE *with the wounded* GUNTHER. *Exit* HAGEN.]

BRÜNNHILDE: [*Alone on stage*] Vassals, build a funeral pyre on the riverbanks!

[*Music cue* 9. BRÜNNHILDE *crosses and stands above the body of the dead* SIEGFRIED, *her hands outstretched.*] Gods, look what you have destroyed!

[*She gently draws the Ring from* SIEGFRIED'*s finger, then places it solemnly on her own hand.*] The Rhinemaidens may soon claim from my ashes this precious Ring, cleansed at last of its curse. [BRÜNNHILDE *crosses and returns with a torch with which she touches the ground and starts the flames. Flames soon engulf the stage.*] Hail, Siegfried!

[BRÜNNHILDE *rushes into the flames, which now burn wildly, and lies beside the body of* SIEGFRIED. *Below, the Rhine overflows. Light reveals the* RHINEMAIDENS, *who now swim happily, holding the Ring. Enter* HAGEN, *he dashes into the flood, as if mad.*]

HAGEN: [*Crying out*] Away from the Ring!

[*The* RHINEMAIDENS *fling their arms around his neck and, swimming away, draw him down with them into the depths. Once* HAGEN *is drowned, the* RHINEMAIDENS *continue to swim, each in turn, holding the Ring. As the Motive of the Rhinemaidens is heard images appear through the flames, in the sky, retelling events from* Die Walküre, Siegfried *and* Götterdämmerung. *As the Motive of Redemption Through Love sounds, a final image of* WOTAN *surrounded by* BRÜNNHILDE, SIEGFRIED, SIEGMUND *and* SIEGLINDE *appear, as if burning in the sky. Clean white light beams onto the real bodies of* SIEGFRIED *and* BRÜNNHILDE *still in the flames center stage. And*

finally, a beam of golden light illuminates the RHINE-
MAIDENS *holding forth the Ring, returned to the Rhine,
cleansed at last of its curse. Lights fade as music fades.*]

CURTAIN
THE END of *Götterdämmerung*

APPENDIX

Musical Excerpts for
THE RING

The selected musical excerpt cues listed within the four plays are coordinated here with page and measure numbers from the operatic piano/vocal scores of *Das Rheingold, Die Walküre, Siegfried* and *Götterdämmerung* published by G. Schirmer.

*Use orchestral recordings without voice.

DAS RHEINGOLD   *Timing*

1. The Rhine River *(over dialogue)*   2.30
        page 2, measure 10
        through page 5, measure 6
        (fade on measures 5 and 6)

2. Introduction to Scene 1 *(Valhalla Motive)*   1.00
        page 55, measure 1
        through page 55, measure 16
        (fade by middle of measure 16)

3. Giants Motive   .12
        page 68, measure 1
        through page 68, measure 3

4. Bridge to Scene 3 *(Nibelungen Motive)*   .30
    page 112, measure 18
    through page 113, measure 13
    (fade on measure 13)

5. Bridge to Scene 4.   .54
    page 158, measure 8
    through page 160, measure 1
    (cut after first beat of measure 1)

6. Erda's Entrance and Motive   .32
    page 192, measure 7
    through page 192, measure 15
    (fade on measure 15)

7. Entrance of the Gods to Valhalla *(End of*   1.12
   Das Rheingold)
    page 221, measure 1
    through to bottom of page

DIE WALKÜRE   *Timing*

1. Introduction to Act I   .54
    page 2, measure 28
    (fade in on second beat of measure 28)
    through page 4, measure 14
    (fade on measure 14)

2. Love Motive   .18
    page 13, measure 13
    through page 13, measure 17
    (fade after first beat of measure 17)

3. Hunding Motive   .07
    page 16, measure 9
    through page 16, measure 10

4. Sword Motive   .09
   page 39, measure 7
   through page 39, measure 10

5. End of Act I   .25
   page 76, measure 15
   through page 77, bottom of page

6. Introduction to Act II   .40
   page 80, measure 9
   through page 81, measure 5
   (cut after first beat of measure 5)

7. Hojotoho   .40
   page 82, measure 2
   (fade in on measure 2)
   through page 83, measure 8
   (fade on measure 8)

8. Entrance of Siegmund and Sieglinde   .20
   page 139, measure 15
   through page 140, measure 1
   (fade on first beat of measure 1)

9. End of Act II   .20
   page 183, measure 3
   through to bottom of page

*10. Ride of the Valkyries *(Introduction to Act III)*   .46
   page 187, measure 9
   (fade in on measure 9)
   through page 189, measure 3
   (fade on measure 3)

11. Magic Fire Music *(End of Die Walküre)*   2.05
   page 303, measure 2
   through page 304, bottom of page

SIEGFRIED   *Timing*

1. Introduction to Act I *(Nibelungen Motive)*   .18
     page 4, measure 24
     through page 5, measure 5
     (cut after first beat of measure 5)

2. Siegfried's Horn Motive   .07
     see: *Götterdämmerung, excerpt 2.*

3. Valhalla Motive *(over dialogue)*   .17
     page 61, measure 22
     through page 62, measure 2
     (fade on last beat of measure 2)
     use: *Das Rheingold, excerpt 2.*
     page 55, measure 1
     through page 55, measure 5
     (fade on triplet)

4. End of Act I   .16
     page 135, measure 14
     through to bottom of page

5. Introduction to Act II *(Fafner Motive)*   .50
     page 136, measure 1
     through page 136, measure 16
     (fade before third beat of measure 16)

6. Forest Murmurs   .35
     page 176, measure 18
     through page 177, measure 11

7. End of Act II   .40
     page 237, measure 10
     (fade in on second half of measure 10)
     through page 238, bottom of page

8. Introduction to Act III   .40
    page 240, measure 16
    through page 241, measure 15
    (fade on measure 15)

9. Bridge to Act III, Scene 1   1.05
    page 281, measure 7
    through page 283, measure 1
    (fade by second half of measure 1)

10. End of Act III   .25
    page 337, measure 9
    through to bottom of page

GÖTTERDÄMMERUNG   *Timing*

1. Introduction to Prologue *(Dawn Duet)*   1.05
    page 20, measure 9
    through page 21, measure 8
    (fade after first beat of measure 8)

2. Siegfried's Rhine Journey   2.35
    page 39, measure 1
    through page 42, measure 8
    (fade on measure 8)

3. Siegfried's Horn Motive   .07
    page 57, measure 7
    through page 57, measure 10

4. Bridge to Act I, Scene 2   1.45
    page 87, measure 21
    through page 88, measure 19

5. End of Act I, Scene 2   .25

      page 128, measure 5
      through to bottom of page

  6. End of Act II *(Wedding Procession)*   .46
      page 229, measure 12
      through page 230, bottom of page

  7. Rhinemaidens and Siegfried *(over dia-*   1.10
      logue)
      page 232, measure 18
      through page 234, measure 1
      (fade after first beat of measure 1)

  8. Siegfried's Funeral Music   2.15
      page 302, measure 19
      (fade in on fourth beat of measure 19)
      through page 304, measure 9
      (fade on fourth beat of measure 9)

 *9. Immolation Scene *(End of*   5.00
      Götterdämmerung)
      page 334, measure 7
      through page 340, bottom of page

Pronouncing Glossary for
THE RING

ALBERICH (AHL-ber-ik), King of the Nibelungs, a dwarf, brother of Mime.

BRÜNNHILDE (Bruen-HILL-da), a Valkyrie.

DONNER (DOHN-ner), The God of Thunder.

ERDA (AIR-dah), The Earth Goddess.

FAFNER (FAHF-ner), a giant in *Das Rheingold,* transformed into a dragon in *Siegfried,* brother of Fasolt.

FASOLT (FAH-sohlt), a giant, brother of Fafner.

FREIA (FRY-ah), The Goddess of Youth and Beauty.

FRICKA (FRIK-ah), The Goddess of Marriage, wife of Wotan.

FROH (FRO), The God of Lightning.

GIBICH (GIBB-ish), Gunther and Gutrune's race.

GIBICHUNG (GIBB-ish-oong), of the race of Gibich (as in Gibichung Hall).

GÖTTERDÄMMERUNG (GOET-ter-DAEM-mer-oong), (Title of fourth play), Twilight of the Gods.

GRANE (GRAH-neh), Brünnhilde's horse.

GUNTHER (GOON-ter), a Gibich, brother of Gutrune.

GUTRUNE (Goot-TROON-eh), a Gibich, sister of Gunther.

HAGEN (HAH-gen), half brother of Gunther, son of Alberich.

HOJOTOHO (HO-yo-to-ho), Brünnhilde's battle cry.

HUNDING (HOON-ding), a Neidung, married to Sieglinde.

LOGE (LOW-geh), The God of Fire.

MIME (MEE-meh), a dwarf, brother of Alberich.

NEIDUNG (NYE-doong), Hunding's tribe.

NIBELUNG (NEE-bel-loong), deep in the earth, a member of the race of Nibelung.

NIBELUNGEN (NEE-bel-loong-en), the race of Nibelung.

RHEINGOLD, DAS (dahss RINE-gold), (Title of first play), The Rhine Gold.

RING DES NIBELUNGEN, DER (dare RING des NEE-bel-loong-en), (collective Title of *Das Rheingold, Die Walküre, Siegfried* and *Götterdämmerung*), The Ring of the Nibelungen, specifically: *Alberich's Ring*.

SIEGFRIED (ZEEG-freed), (Title/character of third play), son of Siegmund and Sieglinde.

SIEGLINDE (zeeg-LIN-da), a Walsung, married to Hunding, long-lost twin sister of Siegmund.

SIEGMUND (ZEEG-moond), a Walsung, long-lost twin brother of Sieglinde.

TARNHELM (TARN-helm), magic helmet made from the Rhine Gold.

VALHALLA (vahl-HALL-ah), The Castle of the Gods built by Fasolt and Fafner.

VALKYRIE (vahl-KEE-ree), a warrior maiden.

WALKÜRE, DIE (dee vahl-KUER-reh), (Title of second play), The Valkyrie, specifically: *Brünnhilde*.

WALSUNG (VELL-soong), Siegmund and Sieglinde's tribe.

WALTRAUTE (vahl-TRAU-ta), a Valkyrie.

WOTAN (VOH-tahn), Ruler of the Gods, disguised as The Wanderer in *Siegfried*.

RING AROUND THE ROSY

by Stephen Wadsworth

There is a new *Ring* cycle. Basically it is a Bayreuth disk raked at ten degrees, but it also resembles the Karajan style, with a *Walküre* tree and a Valkyries' rock straight out of Schneider-Siemssen, while the projection of Ludwig of Bavaria's castle Neuschwanstein as Valhalla in *Rheingold* mirrors the latest vogue in *Ring* stagings—parallels to Wagner's own life. Even more *au courant* is this new production's Chéreauesque need to involve the audience's sensibilities in new ways. Yet the Rhine is represented by undulating fabric, an ancient theatrical illusion. There is also brutal humor that smacks of Punch and Judy, and the action unfolds with the lie-down-and-die inevitability of ritual theater.

The music is played by a variety of orchestras under a variety of conductors, including Solti, and there is no singing. There is, however, a healthy substitute, and that is screaming. Freia screams when the giants drag her off, Sieglinde screams when Siegmund extracts Nothung from the tree, Brünnhilde screams when she sees the ring on Siegfried's hand, and Gutrune screams when the dead Siegfried's arm rises up. The Rhinemaidens, lamenting the theft of the Rhine Gold, howl like little girls over a stolen ball at recess. The act of screaming rivets their bodies, opens wide their mouths and glazes over their eyes, and they look like sopranos singing over a large orchestra.

The great things about this *Ring* are its truthfulness to Wagner and its flexibility. Anyone can do it. You can do this *Ring* with children. In fact, you *must* do it with children, because it was arranged for them to perform. *The Ring* is four children's plays, each about twenty minutes long, adapted from Wagner by Philip Caggiano for a theater-and-music class at the School Settlement Association in Williamsburg, Brooklyn. In Spring 1979 it was produced at the Somers Intermediate School in northern Westchester County, where it became known as the Somers *Ring*.

Caggiano, an aspiring opera director, brought much experience to bear on this enterprise. He has studied voice at Juilliard, toured in musical comedy, taken a degree in education at NYU, dressed windows and served as production designer for several Kung Fu films. He is thin and urbane. "I wrote the plays for kids who had no musical background, who couldn't match pitches. This was really not an opera-education program. I just couldn't find a play that used music I liked, and it was easiest for me to adapt opera stories, because I could knock them off in my mind. I didn't want to take an opera that was originally a play, then do a tacky treatment of it and add music. And I could pull more music from *The Ring* than I could from anywhere else. The children who do these plays have an experience with theater, with Wagner and with how music and theater mix together. So if opera is musical theater, they certainly do learn something about opera, yes."

In April, as part of the five-day Opera America Education Workshop in New York, some of the Somers production was carted into List Hall at the Metropolitan Opera House, where Caggiano introduced highlights, the cast performed them, and the Somers principal, Richard Stock, discussed the project: "I have grayer hair than I did before. Years ago, when I hired Eric Steinman, I did so because he played a great piano. He had other things I didn't know about at the time. One of the things that's evolved in our school has been the study of the opera. Every year Eric selects an opera, and we all go with it. This year the theme of our middle program was *The Ring*. All 650 of us were exposed to it, with help from some of Eric's old friends in the junior and senior high. We put this on in the huge high school auditorium. When you do something in one building and put it on in another, you have some mechanical difficulties, and we overcame these with money. We put the performance on for over a thousand people, and up in Somers that's a pretty good trick. We charged a dollar basically, and three dollars for the best seats, and we came out about even.

"Whenever you do a big project that affects other areas of study, teachers complain. If you just sing Christmas carols, someone complains. Eric has had enough run-ins with the faculty, so we published a monstrous schedule, making sure we didn't pull the same kids from the same class too many times, which is where principals get in trouble. And there was cooperation, especially from the parents. Theater's important. I can remember *The Pirates of Penzance* in seventh grade; what fun it was. I run the school on that basis."

Rooting around among the stars, I found Siegmund and Siegfried in their furs. Do they think they learned anything about music from this play? "Well, I was over at his house and we were watching television," said Siegfried, "and it was some of the music from *The Ring*." "Siegfried's Rhine Journey," interjected Siegmund. A lot of the other kids seemed anxious to try out Wagner's version in the opera house. "I mean, I know the story—nobody knows the story like me." "I think it's long, but I would be patient. I would wait for the redemption theme." "Four nights? Forget it. They should do it on TV. I like opera okay on TV." Caggiano adds with a smile, "We trained Sieglinde's scream on the Rysanek Bayreuth recording. That little girl knows that part *quite* well now."

The Somers *Ring* is often beautiful to look at, and when it's over [in two hours] you feel a scaled-down version of what you feel when the redemption theme sends you out into the dark night at the close of a Bayreuth *Götter-dämmerung*—tired, surfeited with images, moved, sentimental and grand. Caggiano's *Ring* plays are clever, clear accounts of a good story, and extended bits of arching orchestral music sweep the dialogue along at crucial points. Children's voices provide a touching counterpoint. A young soprano next to me said, teary-eyed, "They make me cry, the projections at the end. They really wreck me."

Caggiano is full of the particulars: "I was very careful to be faithful to Wagner. I never pulled music out of other places in the score. I wanted to be humorous but not funny. I tried to write it as one of us might explain an opera story to a friend, paraphrasing what I thought would be a child's vernacular. When you get to key lines, here may be humor—the humor of a Brünnhilde, age twelve, standing over the dead body of Siegfried and saying, 'Gods, look at what you have destroyed!' I wanted to do things that weren't so technically sophisticated that they would take away from the fact that these are after all children doing a children's play. One source that was particularly wonderful is the book illustrated by Arthur Rackham, with that beautiful English verse translation by Margaret Armour. Also in designing the production I wanted to do a dramatization of a children's book, simple and colorful, Beni Montresor-like."

Mounted on that Bayreuth disk with two mobile platforms to vary the setting, the production is framed by projections, first of the Seattle *Ring* logo (suspended perhaps over the basketball hoop, as in Brooklyn), finally of stills from the four plays which retell the story as the Cleveland Orchestra plays the finale over the loudspeakers. The only gimmick is something called The Great American Scene Machine (available from most lighting rentals for about $150 a week), which can create walls of fire, floating clouds and other fine effects with colored lights and an oscillating disc-and-lens system. There are tracks for movable scenery, which is set up by the same hands that operate the river.

In Somers, Caggiano had five assistant directors responsible for props and scene changes, who also took blocking and staging notes at rehearsals and kept a production book with diagrams. The cast of fifty included three adults—as Wotan, Fasolt (Steinman himself) and Fafner (the father of the brother and sister who played Siegmund and Sieglinde). Everyone in Somers was costumed by an intrepid teacher's aid, Helen Webber, for about four dollars each, including fake fur. A parent built the disk, about twenty-three by fifteen feet, and the art teacher supervised the painting of the scenery, which was cut out of Homasote. The ring itself was a plastic curtain-rod ring with a red plastic translucent ponytail ball glued onto it. It is a big ring, and in Somers there were several of them, so elementary stage magic was possible—the Rhinemaidens, for instance, could hold one up instantly when Brünnhilde threw hers into the Great American Scene Machine flames.

There were many fine performances. Mime and Alberich were appropriately foul-faced, Loge was slimy, Gunther spineless and Freia beauteous in her yellow chiffon cocktail dress. Siegfried, a spunky real-life gymnast, and Brünnhilde, an older girl in athletic socks, believed in what they were doing, and their wildly disparate heights (the warrior-goddess was a foot taller than her hero) seemed a thing to rejoice in. Erda was a real find, a funny, round-jowled girl draped in lavender, eerily embodying Anna Russell's "green-faced torso." Alberich snatched the gold to the E-flat susurrations that start *Das Rheingold,* Siegmund's and Sieglinde's eyes met on the love theme, and Siegfried lunched on a turkey leg during the forest murmurs.

And there are great lines. Gods to Wotan, after Freia has been carried off [in woeful unison]: "Wotan, Wotan, do something—we can feel the wrinkles happening!" Brünnhilde to Gutrune [snidely]: *"You* were *never* Siegfried's wife. You were a mere *interloper."* And so on.

—Courtesy of
OPERA NEWS

BARD BOOKS
DISTINGUISHED DRAMA

NEW FROM BARD
DISTINGUISHED MODERN FICTION

HIDING PLACE
John Edgar Wideman   78501 $2.95

This is a moving novel of a runaway young tough, the
old woman he seeks refuge with, and her simple-
minded errand boy on a hilltop high above the Pitts-
burgh ghetto of Homewood, by "the most gifted black
novelist of his generation." *The Nation*

DAMBALLAH
John Edgar Wideman   78519 $2.95

DAMBALLAH is an unsparing portrait of a family and
of the Black experience, in the ghetto founded by a
runaway slave and her white husband. "Wideman can
write. . . . He can make an ordinary scene sing the
blues like nobody's business." *The New York Times*

KINDERGARTEN
Peter Rushforth   56150 $2.95

A family's preparations for Christmas in England con-
trast with grim realities in this novel, winner of England's prestigious Hawthornden literature prize. "A
powerful affirmation of civilization and culture. . . . Mr.
Rushforth has unlocked a forbidden door and exposed
the mutilated remains of childhood's innocence." *The
New York Times*

O MY AMERICA!
Johanna Kaplan   56515 $3.50

Winner of the 1981 National Jewish Book Award, this
follows the life of an American iconoclast, and his
sometimes blurred vision of the American Dream. "O
beautiful for pure perfection. . . . Without faults. . . .
Wonderful." *Philadelphia Inquirer*

THE JUNKERS
Piers Paul Read   56937 $2.95

This provocative novel of international suspense and
romance is set in Berlin, where a young man attempts
to reconcile his love for a beautiful woman with her
family's Nazi past. "A fine achievement." *The Washington Post*

"A masterpiece. . . . One of the best novels of our time . . ."

The New York Times Book Review (front page)

THE BOOK OF

EBENEZER LE PAGE

BY G.B. EDWARDS

Introduction by John Fowles

This novel of a crusty Guernsey Island inhabitant has been acclaimed by reviewers on both sides of the Atlantic as one of the literary finds of the century.

"Breathtaking . . . gripping. . . . The bold assault on our feelings is irresistible."

Newsweek

"It amuses, it entertains, it moves us; it can shift from pain to bawdy humor and back again, effortlessly, as convincing in its tones and shifts as the voice of a worldly, cunning and soulful blues singer. . . . He becomes a universal figure and his story becomes the story of our century."

Washington Post Book World

"A brilliant reminiscence: one man's homage to the simple life . . . (and) the qualities of honesty, integrity, humor and endurance."

Chicago Sun-Times

"The characters, as well as the many remarkable incidents, will long linger in the memory. . . . Ebenezer himself, by turns wise, perceptive, foolish and irascible, is one of the most human characters you will encounter in many a day . . ."

Dallas Morning News